U0111775

大展好書　好書大展
品嘗好書　冠群可期

▲作者的少林拳　Shaolin Boxing of the Author

▲武術雜誌上的耿軍
Geng Jun on the Cover of Wushu Magazine

▲英法武術代表團訪問孟州少林武術院
The Wushu Delegation of France and UK is visiting the Meng zhou Shaolin Wushu Institute

▲作者部分弟子參加武打片拍攝
Parts of students of author take part in fliming Acrobatic fighting film

▲作者與恩師素法大師
The Author and his Teacher Grandmaster Sufa

▲作者指導女兒耿瑞濤練功
The Author is coaching his daughter to practise her skill

▲作者與原國家武術協會主席張耀庭
The Author and the former Chairman of the Chinese Wushu
Association Zhang Yaoting

▲作者的少林拳　Shaolin Boxing of the Author

▲ 武術雜誌封面上的耿軍
Geng Jun on the Cover of Wushu Magazine

▲ 作者與恩師素法大師
The Author and his Teacher Grandmaster Sufa

▲ 作者率領國外弟子朝拜少林寺　Author leads foreign students to visit Shaolin Temple

▲作者與武僧教頭德揚師兄在捶譜堂
In Chuipu Hall, the author and his senior fellow apprentice
who is also the wushu monk teacher deyang

▲作者與中國政協副主席萬國權
The Author and the vice Chairman of the Chinese People's Political
Consultative Conference（CPPCC）Wan Guoquan

▲作者傳藝國際黑帶功夫總會
The Author is teaching his Wushu skill in International
Black Belt Kungfu Federation

▲作者指導兒子耿鵬飛練功
The Author is coaching his son Geng Pengfei to practise
his skill

少林傳統功夫漢英對照系列　④

Shaolin Traditional Kungfu Series Books　④

七星螳螂拳

Seven–star Mantis Boxing（insert Boxing）

插捶

耿　軍　著

Written by Geng Jun

大展出版社有限公司

作者簡介

耿軍（法號釋德君），1968 年 11 月出生於河南省孟州市，係少林寺三十一世皈依弟子。中國武術七段、全國十佳武術教練員、中國少林武術研究會副秘書長、焦作市政協十屆常委、濟南軍區特警部隊特邀武功總教練、洛陽師範學院客座教授、英才教育集團董事長。1989 年創辦孟州少林武術院、2001 年創辦英才雙語學校。先後獲得河南省優秀青年新聞人物、全國優秀武術教育家等榮譽稱號。

1983 年拜在少林寺住持素喜法師和著名武僧素法大師門下學藝，成爲大師的關門弟子，後經素法大師引薦，又隨螳螂拳一代宗師李占元、金剛力功于憲華等大師學藝。在中國鄭州國際少林武術節、全國武林精英大賽、全國武術演武大會等比賽中 6 次獲得少林武術冠軍；在中華傳統武術精粹大賽中獲得了象徵少林武術最高榮譽的「達摩杯」一座。他主講示範的 36集《少林傳統功夫》教學片已由人民體育音像出版社出版發行。他曾多次率團出訪海外，在國際武術界享有較高聲譽。

　　他創辦的孟州少林武術院，現已發展成爲豫北地區最大的以學習文化爲主、以武術爲辦學特色的封閉式、寄宿制學校，是中國十大武術教育基地之一。

Brief Introduction to the Author

作
者
簡
介

Geng Jun〔also named Shidejun in Buddhism〕, born in Mengzhou City of Henan Province, November 1968, is a Bud-dhist disciple of the 31st generation, the 7th section of Chinese Wu shu, national "Shijia" Wu shu coach, Vice Secretary General of China Shaolin Wu shu Research Society, standing committee member of 10th Political Consultative Conference of Jiaozuo City, invited General Kungfu Coach of special police of Jinan Military District, visiting professor of Luoyang Normal University, and Board Chairman of Yingcai Education Group. In 1989, he estab-lished Mengzhou Shaolin Wu shu Institute; in 2001, he estab-lished Yingcai Bilingual School · He has been successively awarded honorable titles of "Excellent Youth News Celebrity of Henan Province" "State Excellent Wu shu Educationalist" etc.

In 1983, he learned Wu shu from Suxi Rabbi, the Abbot of Shaolin Temple, and Grandmaster Sufa, a famous Wu shu monk, and became the last disciple of the

Grandmaster. Then recom–mended by Grandmaster Sufa, he learned Wu shu from masters such as Li Zhanyuan, great master of mantis boxing, and Yu Xianhua who specializes in Jingangli gong. He won the Shaolin Wu shu champion for 6 times in China Zhengzhou International Wu shu Festival, National Competition of Wu lin Elites, National Wu shu Performance Conference, etc. and one "Damo Trophy" that symbolizes the highest honor of Shaolin Wu shu in Chinese Traditional Wu shu Succinct Competition. 36 volumes teaching VCD of Shaolin Traditional Wu shu has been published and is –sued by People´s Sports Audio Visual Publishing House. He has led delegations to visit overseas for many times, enjoying high reputation in the martial art circle of the world.

Mengzhou Shaolin Wu shu Institute, established by him, has developed into the largest enclosed type boarding school of Yubei (north of Henan Province) area, which takes knowledge as primary and Wu shu as distinctiveness, also one of China´s top ten Wu shu education bases.

序　言

　　中華武術源遠流長，門類繁多。

　　少林武術源自嵩山少林寺，因寺齊名，是我國拳系中著名的流派之一。少林寺自北魏太和十九年建寺以來，已有一千五百多年的歷史。而少林武術也決不是哪一人哪一僧所獨創，它是歷代僧俗歷經漫長的生活歷程，根據生活所需逐步豐富完善而成。

　　據少林寺志記載許多少林僧人在出家之前就精通武術或慕少林之名而來或迫於生計或看破紅塵等諸多原因削髮爲僧投奔少林，少林寺歷來倡武，並經常派武僧下山，雲遊四方尋師學藝。還請武林高手到寺，如宋朝的福居禪師曾邀集十八家武林名家到寺切磋技藝，推動了少林武術的發展，使少林武術得諸家之長。

　　本書作者自幼習武，師承素喜、素法和螳螂拳李占元等多位名家，當年如饑似渴在少林寺研習功夫，曾多次在國內外大賽中獲獎。創辦的孟州少林武術院亦是全國著名的武術院校之一，他示範主講的 36 集《少林傳統功夫》教學 VCD 已由人民體育音像出版社發行。

　　本套叢書的三十多個少林傳統套路和實戰技法是少

林武術的主要內容，部分還是作者獨到心得，很值得一讀，該書還採用漢英文對照，使外國愛好者無語言障礙，爲少林武術走向世界做出了自己的貢獻，亦是可喜可賀之事。

張耀庭題

甲申秋月

Preface

Chinese Wushu is originated from ancient time and has a long history, it has various styles.

Shaolin Wushu named from the Shaolin Temple of Songshan Mountain, it is one of the famous styles in the Chinese boxing genre. Shaolin temple has more than 1500 years of history since its establishment in the 19th year of North Wei Taihe Dynasty. No one genre of Shaolin Wushu is created solely by any person or monk, but completed gradually by Buddhist monks and common people from generation to generation through long-lasting living course according to the requirements of life. As recording of Record of Shaolin Temple, many Shaolin Buddhist monks had already got a mastery of Wushu before they became a Buddhist monk, they came to Shaolin for tonsure to be a Buddhist monk due to many reasons such as admiring for the name of Shaolin, or by force of life or seeing through thevanity of life. The Shaolin Temple always promotes Wushu and frequently appoints Wushu Buddhist monks to go down the mountain to roam around for searching masters and learning Wushu from them. It also invites

Wushu experts to come to the temple, such as Buddhist monk Fuju of Song Dynasty, it once invited Wushu famous exports of 18 schools to come to the temple to make skill interchange, which promoted the development of Shaolin Wushu and made it absorb advantages of all other schools.

The author learned from many famous exports such as Suxi, Sufa and Li Zhanyuan of Mantis Boxing, he studied Chinese boxing eagerly in Shaolin Temple, and got lots of awards both at home and abroad, he also set up the Mengzhou Shaolin Wushu Institute, which is one of the most famous Wushu institutes around China. He makes demonstration and teaching in the 36 volumes teaching VCD of Shaolin Traditional Wushu, which have been published by Peoples sports Audio Visual publishing house.

There are more than 30 traditional Shaolin routines and practical techniques in this series of books, which are the main content of Shaolin Wushu, and part of which is the original things learned by the author, it is worthy of reading. The series books adopt Chinese and English versions, make foreign fans have no language barrier, and make contribution to Shaolin Wushu going to the world, which is delighting and congratulating thing.

Titled by Zhang Yaoting

目 錄
Contents

七星螳螂拳　插捶

説　明

　　（一）為了表述清楚，以圖像和文字對動作作了分解說明，練習時應力求連貫銜接。

　　（二）在文字說明中，除特別說明外，不論先寫或後寫身體的某一部分，各運動部位都要求協調活動、連貫銜接，切勿先後割裂。

　　（三）動作方向轉變以人體為準，標明前後左右。

　　（四）圖上的線條是表明這一動作到下一動作經過的線路及部位。左手、左腳及左轉均為虛線（┈┈▶）；右手、右腳及右轉均為實線（──▶）。

Instructions

(i) In order to explain clearly figures and words are used to describe the actions in multi steps. Try to keep coherent when exercising.

(ii) In the word instruction, unless special instruction, each action part of the body shall act harmoniously and join coherently no matter it is written first or last, please do not separate the actions.

(iii) The action direction shall be turned taking body as standard, which is marked with front, back, left or right.

(iv) The line in the figure shows the route and position from this action to the next action. The left hand, left foot and turn left are all showed in broken line (-----►) ; the right hand, right foot and turn right are all showed in real line (——►) .

基本步型與基本手型
Basic stances and Basic hand forms

圖 1

圖 2

圖 3

圖 4

圖 5

圖 6

圖 7

圖 8

圖 9

圖 10

圖 11

圖 12

基本步型與基本手型

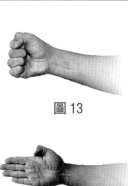

圖 13

圖 14

圖 15

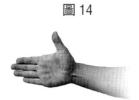

圖 16

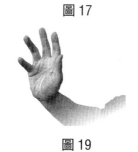

圖 17

圖 18

圖 19

圖 20

圖 21

基本步型

少林武術中常見的步型有：弓步、馬步、仆步、虛步、歇步、坐盤步、丁步、併步、七星步、跪步、高虛步、翹腳步12種。

弓步：俗稱弓箭步。兩腿前後站立，兩腳相距本人腳長的4～5倍；前腿屈至大腿接近水平，腳尖微內扣不超過5°；後腿伸膝挺直，腳掌內扣45°。（圖1）

馬步：俗稱騎馬步。兩腳開立，相距本人腳長的3～3.5倍，兩腳尖朝前；屈膝下蹲大腿接近水平，膝蓋與兩腳尖上下成一條線。（圖2）

仆步：俗稱單叉，一腿屈膝全蹲，大腿貼緊小腿，膝微外展，另一腿直伸平仆接近地面，腳掌扣緊與小腿成90°夾角。（圖3）

虛步：又稱寒雞步。兩腳前後站立，前後相距本人腳長的2倍；重心移至後腿，後腿屈膝下蹲至大腿接近水平，腳掌外擺45°；前腿腳尖點地，兩膝相距10公分。（圖4）

歇步：兩腿左右交叉，靠近全蹲；前腳全腳掌著地，腳尖外展，後腳腳前掌著地，臀部微坐於後腿小腿上。（圖5）

坐盤步：在歇步的形狀下，坐於地上，後腿的大小腿外側和腳背均著地。（圖6）

　　丁步：兩腿併立，屈膝下蹲，大腿接近水平，一腳尖點地靠近另一腳內側腳窩處。（圖7）

　　併步：兩腿併立，屈膝下蹲，大腿接近水平。（圖8）

　　七星步：七星步是少林七星拳和大洪拳中獨有的步型。一腳內側腳窩內扣於另一腳腳尖，兩腿屈膝下蹲，接近水平。（圖9）

　　跪步：又稱小蹬山步。兩腳前後站立，相距本人腳長的2.5倍，前腿屈膝下蹲，後腿下跪，接近地面，後腳腳跟離地。（圖10）

　　高虛步：又稱高點步。兩腳前後站立，重心後移，後腿腳尖外擺45°，前腿腳尖點地，兩腳尖相距一腳距離。（圖11）

　　翹腳步：在七星螳螂拳中又稱七星步，兩腿前後站立，相距本人腳長的1.5倍，後腳尖外擺45°，屈膝下蹲，前腿直伸，腳跟著地，腳尖微內扣。（圖12）

基本手型

少林武術中常見的手型有拳、掌、鈎3種。

　　拳：

分為平拳和透心拳。

　　平拳：平拳是武術中較普遍的一種拳型，又稱方拳。四指屈向手心握緊，拇指橫屈扣緊食指。（圖

13）

透心拳：此拳主要用於打擊心窩處，故名。四指併攏捲握，中指突出拳面，拇指扣緊抵壓中指梢節處。（圖14）

掌：

分為柳葉掌、八字掌、虎爪掌、鷹爪掌、鉗指掌。

柳葉掌：四指併立，拇指內扣。（圖15）

八字掌：四指併立，拇指張開。（圖16）

虎爪掌：五指分開，彎曲如鉤，形同虎爪。（圖17）

鷹爪掌：又稱鎖喉手，拇指內扣，小指和無名指彎曲扣於掌心處，食指和中指分開內扣。（圖18）

鉗指掌：五指分開，掌心內含。（圖19）

鉤：

分為鉤手和螳螂鉤。

鉤手：屈腕，五指自然內合，指尖相攏。此鉤使用較廣，武術中提到的鉤均為此鉤。（圖20）

螳螂鉤：又稱螳螂爪，屈腕成腕部上凸，無名指、小指屈指內握，食指、中指內扣，拇指梢端按貼於食指中節。（圖21）

Basic stances

Usual stances in Shaolin Wushu are: bow stance, horse stance, crouch stance, empty stance, rest stance, cross – legged sitting, T – stance, feet – together stance, seven – star stance, kneel stance, high empty stance, and toes – raising stance, these twelve kinds.

Bow stance: commonly named bow – and – arrow stance. Two feet stand in tandem, the distance between two feet is about four or five times of length of one´s foot; the front leg bends to the extent of the thigh nearly horizontal with toes slightly turned inward by less than 5°; the back leg stretches straight with the sole turned inward by 45°. (Figure 1)

Horse stance: commonly named riding step. two feet stand apart, the distance between two feet is 3~3.5 times of length of one´s foot, with tiptoes turned forward; bend knees to squat downward, with thighs nearly horizontal, knees and two tiptoes in line. (Figure 2)

Crouch stance: commonly named single split. Bend the knee of one leg and squat entirely with thigh very close to lower leg and knee outspread slightly; straighten the other leg and crouch horizontally close to floor, keep the sole turned inward and forming an included angle of 90° with lower leg. (Figure 3)

Empty stance: also named cold – chicken stance. Two feet stand in tandem, the distance between two feet is 2 times of

length of one´s foot; transfer the barycenter to back leg, bend the knee of the back leg and squat downward to the extent of the thigh nearly horizontal, with the sole turned outward by 45°; keep the tiptoe of front leg on the ground, with distance between two knees of 10cm. (Figure 4)

Rest stance: cross the two legs at left and right, keep them close and entirely squat; keep the whole sole of the front foot on the ground with tiptoes turned outward, the front sole of the back foot on the ground, and buttocks slightly seated on the lower leg of the back leg. (Figure 5)

Cross–legged sitting: in the posture of rest stance, sit on the ground, with the outer sides of the thigh and lower leg of the back leg and instep on the ground. (Figure 6)

T–stance: two legs stand with feet together, bend knees and squat to the extent of the thighs nearly horizontal, with one tiptoe on the ground and close to inner side of the fossa of the other foot. (Figure 7)

Feet–together stance: two legs stand with feet together, bend knees and squat to the extent of the thigh nearly horizontal. (Figure 8)

Seven–star stance: Seven–star step is a unique step form in Shaolin Seven–star Boxing and Major Flood Boxing. Keep the inner side of the fossa of one foot turned inward onto tiptoe of the other foot, bend two knees and squat nearly horizontal. (Figure 9)

Kneel stance: also named small mountaineering stance. Two feet stand in tandem, the distance between two feet is 2.5

times of length of one's foot, bend knee of the front leg and squat, kneel the back leg close to the floor, with the heel of back foot off the floor. (Figure 10)

High empty stance: also named high point stance. Two feet stand in tandem. Transfer the barycenter backward, turn the tiptoe of the back leg outward by 45°, with tiptoe of front leg on the ground, and the distance between two tiptoes is length of one foot. (Figure 11)

Toes –raising stance: also named seven –star stance in Seven–star Mantis Boxing. Two legs stand in tandem, and the distance between two legs is 1.5 times of length of one's foot. Keep the tiptoe of back leg turned outward by 45°, bend knees and squat, straighten the front leg with heel on the ground and tiptoe turned inward slightly. (Figure 12)

Basic hand forms

Usual hand forms in Shaolin Wushu are: fist, palm and hook, these three kinds.

Fist: classified into straight fist and heart–penetrating fist.

Flat fist: a rather common fist form in Wushu, also named square fist. Hold the four fingers tightly toward the palm, and horizontally bend the thumb to button up the fore finger. (Figure 13)

Heart –penetrating fist: mainly used for striking the heart part. Put four fingers together and coil –hold them, the middle finger thrusts out the striking surface of the fist, the thumb buttons up and presses the end and joint of the middle finger. (Figure 14)

Palm: classified into willow leaf palm, splay palm, tiger's claw palm, eagle's claw palm, fingers clamping palm.

Willow leaf palm: palm with four fingers up and thumb turned inward. (Figure 15)

Eight–shape palm: palm with four fingers up and thumb splay. (Figure 16)

Tiger's claw palm: palm with five fingers apart, bent as hook and like tiger's claw. (Figure 17)

Eagle's claw palm: also named throat locking hand, with the thumb turned inward, the little finger and middle finger turned onto palm, fore finger and middle finger apart and turned inward. (Figure 18)

Fingers clamp palm: palm with five fingers apart and palm drawn in. (Figure 19)

Hook: classified into hook hand and mantis hook.

Hook hand: bend the wrist, five fingers drawn in naturally with fingertips together. This hook is used in wide range, the hook mentioned in Wushu refers to this. (Figure 20)

Mantis hook: also named mantis' claw, bend wrist into wrist bulge upward, the ring finger and little finger bend to hold inward, with fore finger and fore middle finger turned inward and end of thumb pressed on the middle joint of the fore finger. (Figure 21)

插捶套路簡介

Brief Introduction to the Routine Insert Boxing

七星螳螂拳是清初拳師王郎在研究螳螂捕蟬時運用兩臂劈、砍、刁、閃的捕鬥技巧而創編的一種象形拳法。後王郎入少林寺 3 年，向寺僧傳授螳螂拳法。插捶是七星螳螂拳其中的一個套路，該套路剛柔並濟、長短互用、手到腳到、貫穿緊湊、節奏明快、勁整力圓、周身相合、勾摟纏封、變化無窮。

Seven–star mantis boxing is a kind of shape–simulating boxing, which was developed and compiled by Wang Lang, a boxer at early Qing Dynasty, applying the capturing and fighting skills of the two arms when he researched the scene of mantis capturing cicada. Later, Wang Lang stayed at Shao Temple for 3 years, and taught mantis boxing to the monks of this temple. Insert boxing is one of the routines in seven–star mantis boxing, which uses the temper force with grace, both long and short actions, harmonious and consistent actions of the hands and feet, forthright rhythm, integral strength and complete force, the actions of hook, grad, twining and closing, being coherent, compact and most changeful.

插捶套路動作名稱

Action Names of Routine Insert Boxing

第一段　Section One

1. 預備勢　Preparatory posture
2. 上步推掌　Step forward and push palms
3. 插花掌　Ikebana palm
4. 撲食　Spring on prey
5. 摟打一捶　Brush and punch
6. 虎抱頭　Tiger holds head
7. 劈砸圈捶　Chop, pound and circle hammer
8. 挑打窩肚捶　Parry and punch the stomach
9. 跺子腳　Battlement foot
10. 盤肘崩捶連環戳　Hook elbow, snap hammer and jab continuously

第二段　Section Two

11. 轉身掄劈圈捶　Turn, swing, chop and circle hammer
12. 掄劈砸拳　Swing, chop and pound with fist
13. 插花掌　Ikebana palm

14. 抹眉插掌撩陰腳　Smear eyebrow, insert palm and up-percut groin with foot

15. 撲食　Spring on prey

16. 摟打一捶　Brush and punch

17. 轉身一捶　Turn body and thrust hammer

18. 插步盤肘　Insert step and bend elbow

第三段　Section Three

19. 劈挑栽捶　Chop, uppercut and insert hammer

20. 上步雙封圈捶　Step forward, close up hands and circle hammer

21. 裏摟採三手　Brush inward and grab hand three times

22. 撩陰腳　Uppercut-groin foot

23. 順手牽羊　Lead away a goat in passing

24. 左右圈捶　Left and right circular hammer

25. 摟打一捶　Brush and punch

26. 虎抱頭劈砸　Tiger holds head with chop and pound

27. 白鶴亮翅　White crane spreads wings

28. 轉身十字手　Turn body and cross hands

29. 七星捶　Seven-star hammer

第四段　Section Four

30. 摟打躍步捶　Brush and punch with jumping step

七星螳螂拳 插捶

31. 左封右崩捶   Left wrap and right snap hammer
32. 彎弓射虎   Bend bow to shoot the tiger
33. 劈拳   Chop with the fist
34. 左封右崩捶   Left wrap and right snap hammer
35. 雙封手   Close-up double hands
36. 收勢   Closing form

插捶套路動作圖解
Action Illustrtion of Routine Insert Boxing

圖 1

第一段 Section One

1. 預備勢 Preparatory posture

(1)兩腳併立;兩手自然下垂,五指併攏,貼於體側;目視前方。(圖 1)

(1) Stand with feet together. Two hands hang na-turally, five fingers put together and stick to both sides of the body. Eyes look forward.〔Figure 1〕

七星螳螂拳　插捶

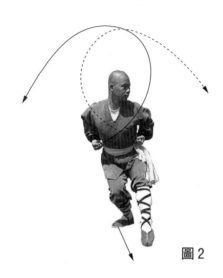

圖2

　　(2)左腳向身體前方上半步，腳尖點地，右腿屈膝成左虛步；同時，兩手變拳上提，抱於兩腰間；目視左方。（圖2）

　　(2) The left foot takes a half-step toward the front of the body, tiptoes land to ground, bend knee of the right leg into the left empty stance. At the same time, change two hands into fists and lift up, hold on the waist. Eyes look leftward.（Figure 2）

圖 3

2. 上步推掌　Step forward and push palms

(1)接上勢。重心前移，左腳踏實，右腳向前上一步；同時，兩拳變掌，經胸前交叉向上舉於頭頂，隨即向身體兩側分掌，兩臂平伸成一直線，兩掌心均向外，掌指均向上；目視右掌。（圖3）

(1)Follow the above posture, shift the barycenter for–ward, the left foot lands firmly, the right foot takes a step forward. At the same time, change two fists into palms, cross through the front of the chest and uplift overhead, then part two palms toward two sides of the body. Two arms stretch horizontally in one line, with two palms outward, the fingers up. Eyes look at the right palm.〔Figure 3〕

圖 4

（2）上動不停。左腳向右腳內側併步；同時，兩掌下落變拳，收抱於腰間，兩拳心均向上；目視前方。（圖 4）

(2) Follow the above posture, bring the left foot to the inner side of the right foot. At the same time, two palms fall down into fists and hold on the waist, with two fist−palm up. Eyes look forward.（Figure 4）

圖5

(3)上動不停。下身姿勢不變；左拳變掌，從腰間
向前平推，掌心向前，掌指向上，高與肩平；目視左
掌。（圖5）

(3) Follow the above posture, keep the posture of the lower
part of the body unchangeable, change the left fist into palm and
horizontally push forward from the waist, with the palm forward
and the fingers up at the shoulder height. Eyes look at the left
palm.（Figure 5）

七星螳螂拳　插捶

圖6

3. 插花掌　Ikebana palm

接上勢。身體向左轉 90°，左腳向前上一步，重心前移成左弓步；同時，右拳變掌，從後向前掄臂砍掌，掌心向左，掌指向前，高與肩平；左臂屈肘收於胸前，左掌變拳貼於右肘下，拳心向下，拳面向右；目視右掌。（圖6）

Follow the above posture, the body turns 90° to the left, the left foot steps forward, move the barycenter forward into the left bow stance. At the same time, change the right fist into palm, and swing arm to chop from back to front, with the palm leftward and the fingers forward at the shoulder height. Bend the left arm and draw it back in front of the chest; change the left palm into fist under the right elbow, with the fist –palm down and the fist –plane out ward. Eyes look at the right palm. (Figure 6)

圖7

4. 撲食　Spring on prey

(1)接上勢。右腳抬起，向左腳跟後方上步震腳；同時，左拳變掌，兩掌在胸前翻轉絞手，抓握成拳，交叉於胸前，右拳心向上，左拳心向下；目視兩拳。（圖7）

(1) Follow the above posture, the right foot lifts up, steps forward toward back of the left heel and stamps the foot. At the same time, change the left fist into palm, turn over two palms in front of the chest and twist hand, clench into fists, cross in front of the chest, with the right fist – palm up and the left one down. Eyes look at two fists.（Figure 7）

挿捶套路動作圖解

圖 8

(2)上動不停。身體右轉 90°，左腳向左鏟腿平仆成左仆步；同時，右拳收抱於腰間，拳心向上；左臂屈肘，向下按拳，置於左小腿內側，拳心向下，拳眼斜向右；目視左拳。（圖 8）

(2)Follow the above posture, the body turns 90° to the right, the left foot shovels leftward and crouch forward into the left crouch stance. At the same time, hold the right fist on the waist, with the fist–palm up; bend elbow of the left arm, Push the left fist downward and put it on the inner side of the left lower leg, with the fist–palm down, the fist–hole rightward aslant. Eyes look at the left fist.〔Figure 8〕

七星螳螂拳 插捶

圖 9

5. 摟打一捶　Brush and punch

　　接上勢。身體左轉 90°，重心前移成左弓步；同時，左拳變掌外摟，隨即抓握變拳收抱於腰間，拳心向上；右拳從腰間向前平沖，拳心向下，拳面向前，高與肩平。（圖 9）

插
捶
套
路
動
作
圖
解

Follow the above posture, the body turns 90° to the left, shift the barycenter forward into the left bow stance. At the same time, change the left fist into palm and brush outward, then clench into fist and hold on the waist, with the fist－palm up; punch the right fist forward horizontally from the waist, with the fist－palm down, the fist－plane forward at the shoulder height. (Figuer 9)

圖 10

6. 虎抱頭　Tiger holds head

接上勢。身體提起，重心前移，左腿獨立，右腳向前蹬出；同時，右臂屈肘，經胸前向上抬起，架拳於頭上方，拳面斜向上，拳眼向下；左拳變掌，從腰間向前平推，掌心向前，掌指向上，高與肩平；目視左掌。（圖 10）

插捶套路動作圖解

Follow the above posture, the body lifts, shift the barycenter forward, the left leg stands alone, the right foot kicks forward. At the same time, bend elbow of the right arm and lift upward through the front of the chest, fist parries above the head, with the fist–plane up aslant, the fist–hole down; change the left fist into palm and push forward horizontally from the waist, with the palm forward and the fingers up at the shoulder height. Eyes look at the left palm. (Figure 10)

圖 11

7. 劈砸圈捶
Chop, pound and circle hammer

（1）接上勢。身體左轉 90°，右腳落地，身體下蹲成馬步；同時，右拳屈肘向身體右側砸拳，置於右膝外側上方，拳輪向下，拳心向前；左掌從下向上迎擊右前臂，掌心貼於右肘關節內側，掌指向上；目視右拳。（圖 11）

插捶套路動作圖解

(1) Follow the above posture, the body turns 90° to the left, the right foot falls to the ground, the body squats down into the horse stance. At the same time, the right fist bend elbow and pound toward the right side of the body to the upper part of the outer side of the right knee, with the fist–wheel down, the fist– palm forward; the left palm counterpunches the right forearm from up to down, with the palm sticking to the inner side of the right elbow joint, the fingers up. Eyes look at the right fist. (Figure 11)

圖12

(2)上動不停。身體提起，略向右轉，重心移至左腿，右腳經左腿內側以腳跟擦地向前撥踢，腳尖向上；同時，右拳向前、向外格肘；左掌附於右肘內側，掌心向下，掌指觸及右肘內側；目視右方。（圖12、圖12附圖）

圖 12 附圖

(2) Keep the above action, uplift the body and turn to the right slightly, shift the barycenter to the left leg, the left foot does wave kick forward with the heel through the inner side of the left leg, with the tiptoe up. At the same time, the right fist swings forward and parry the elbow outward. Attach the left palm to the inner side of the right elbow with the palm down, the fingers touching the inner side of the right elbow. Eyes look rightward. (Figure 12, Attached figure 12)

圖13

(3)上動不停。身體略向左轉，右腳向右後方撤步
成左弓步；同時，右臂屈肘，右拳從外向裏圈擊，拳
心向下，拳面向左，高與肩平；左掌向外劃弧後再向
裏迎擊右前臂，掌指向上，掌心貼於右肘內側；目視
右拳。（圖13、圖13附圖）

要點：整個動作要連貫協調。格肘時擰腰發力，
力達右前臂外側，圈捶時要勁力完整，力達拳面。

插捶套路動作圖解

圖 13 附圖

(3) Keep the above action, the body turns to the left slightly, the right foot takes a step right back into the left bow stance. At the same time, bend the elbow of the right arm, the right fist strikes circularly inward from outside, with the fist–palm down, the fist –plane leftward at the shoulder height; the left palm draws a curve outward and counterpunch the right forearm inward, with the fingers up, the palm sticking to the inner side of the right elbow. Eyes look at the right fist. (Figure 13, Attached figure 13)

Key points: the whole action shall be coherent and consistent, when parrying the elbow, twist the waist to give the strength, which reaches the outer side of the right forearm. When pounding circularly, the force shall be complete and reach the fist–plane.

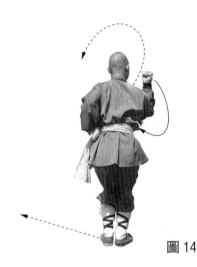

圖 14

8. 挑打窩肚捶
Parry and punch the stomach

(1)接上勢。重心前移，右腳提起，向左腳內側震腳併步，身體下蹲成蹲步；同時，左掌變拳收抱於腰間，拳心向上；右前臂外旋，向右格肘，右拳眼向右，拳心向後，高與頷平；目視右拳。（圖 14）

插捶套路動作圖解

(1)Follow the above posture, shift the barycenter for–ward, the right foot lifts to stamp foot and bring the foot toward the inner side of the left foot, squat the body into the squat stance. At the same time, change the left palm into fist and hold on the waist, with the fist–palm up; the right forearm whirls outward for rightward elbow, with right fist –hole rightward, the fist – palm backward at the chin height. Eyes look at the right fist.
(Figure 14)

圖 15

(2)上動不停。身體左轉 45°，左腳向前跨一步成
左弓步；同時，左拳經胸前上挑並向外格肘，拳心向
後，拳眼向左；右拳向後回環一圈並向前下方沖拳，
拳心向左，拳眼向上；目視右拳。（圖 15、圖 15 附
圖）

要點：蹲步迅速穩固，大腿接近水平，格肘力達
前臂外沿；右拳沖出後自然彈回。

圖 15 附圖

(2) Keep the above action, the body turns 45° to the left, the left foot strides a step forward into the left bow stance. At the same time, the left fist lifts and parry the elbow outward through the front of the chest, with the fist–palm backward and the fist–hole leftward; the right fist returns one circle backward and strikes forward down, with the fist–plam leftward and the fist–hole up. Eyes look at the right fist. (Figure 15, attached figure 15)

Key points: Squat stance shall be quick and stable, the thigh shall be close to the horizontal; the strength of parry elbow reaches the outer side of the right forearm; after striking forward, rebound the fist naturally.

七星螳螂拳　插捶

圖 16

9. 跺子腳　Battlement foot

接上勢。身體提起，重心移至左腿，右腳迅即向左前方下跺，腳跟離地，腳尖勾起；同時，左臂屈肘向下、向外格肘；右臂屈肘向上、向外格肘；左拳置於左胯，右拳置於右肩前上方，兩拳心均向後；目視左方。（圖 16、圖 16 附圖）

要點：跺腳與格肘要同時完成，協調一致，勁力通達。

插捶套路動作圖解

圖 16 附圖

Follow the above posture, lift the body, shift the barycenter to the left leg, then the right foot stamps left forward, with the heel above the ground, the tiptoe up. At the same time, bend elbow of the left arm for downward, outward parry with elbow. Put the left fist on the left hip, put the right fist over the upper part in front of the right shoulder, with two fist –palms backward. Eyes look leftward. (Figure 16, attached figure 16)

Key points: stamping feet and parrying with elbow shall be completed consistently at the same time, with the force applying smoothly.

七星螳螂拳　插捶

圖 17

10. 盤肘崩捶連環戳
Hook elbow, snap hammer and jab continuously

(1)接上勢。身體左轉 90°，右腳向後撤一步成左弓步；同時，右臂屈肘向前盤肘；左拳變掌，向裏迎擊右前臂，掌指向右，掌心貼於右肘外側；目視右肘。（圖 17）

(1) Follow the above posture, the body turns 90° to the left, the right foot takes a step backward and change into the left bow stance. At the same time, bend elbow of the right arm forward to strike with elbow; change the left fist into palm and counterpunch the right forearm inward, with the fingers rightward, the palm sticking to the outer side of the right elbow. Eyes look at the right elbow. (Figure 17)

圖 18

（2）上動不停。身體右轉 180°，右腳向前上半步，左腳隨即跟步；同時，左掌封抓變拳，拳心向下，拳面向前，高與肩平；右拳收抱於腰間，拳心向上；目視左拳。（圖 18）

(2) Keep the above action, the body turns 180° to the right, the right foot takes a half step forward, then the left foot follows up. At the same time, the left palm wraps into fist, with the fist – palm down and the fist –plane forward at the shoulder height; draw back the right fist on the waist, with the fist–palm up. Eyes look at the left fist.〔 Figure 18 〕

圖19

　(3)上動不停。身略左轉下蹲成蹬山步；同時，左
拳屈臂回收；右拳經左前臂內側向前崩拳，拳背向
前，拳眼向右，高與頷平；左拳背貼於右肘下，拳面
向右；目視右拳。（圖19）

(3) Keep the above action, the body turns to the left slightly
and squats into the mountaineer stance. At the same time, bend
the left arm and draw back the left fist; the right fist snaps
forward through the inner side of the left forearm, with the fist –
back forward, the fist –hole rightward at the chin height. Keep
the left fist back sticking under the right elbow, with the fist –
plane rightward. Eyes look at the right fist.（Figure 19）

圖 20

（4）上動不停。左右步交換成左弓步；同時，右拳變掌外摟再收抱於腰間；左拳變掌封抓屈肘成拳，拳心向下，拳面向前，高與肩平；目視左拳。（圖 20）

(4) Keep the above action, change the left –right step into the left bow stance. At the same time, change the right fist into palm, draw back and hold on the waist; the left fist changs into palm and wraps, bend the elbow into fist with the fist –palm down, the fist –plane forward at the shoulder height. Eyes look at the left fist.（Figure 20）

圖 21

(5)上動不停。雙腳步型不變；右拳向前平沖拳，拳心向下，拳面向前，高與肩平；目視右拳。（圖21）

(5) Keep the above action, keep the posture of the two feet unchangeable, The right fist strikes forward horizontally, with the fist -palm down, the fist -plane forward at the shoulder height. Eyes look at the right fist.（Figure 21）

七星螳螂拳　插捶

圖 22

　　⑹上動不停。身體略向右轉，重心後移成玉環步；同時，左拳向前、向上抄拳，拳心向後，拳面向上，高與頜平；右拳變為螳螂鉤向後勾拉，鉤尖向下，置於右肩前；目視左拳。（圖 22）

挿捶套路動作圖解

(6) Keep the above action, the body turns to the right slightly, shift the barycenter back and change into jade –ring step. At the same time, the left fist lifts forward and upward, with the fist –palm backward, the fist –plane up at the chin height; change the right fist into the mantis hook and pull backward, with the hook tip down and put it in front of the right shoulder. Eyes look at the left fist. (Figure 22)

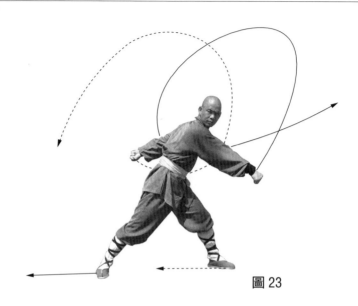

圖 23

第二段　　Section　Two

11. 轉身掄劈圈捶
Turn, swing, chop and circle hammer

(1)接上勢。左腳踏實，身體提起，略向左轉；同時，左拳向下、向後掄臂，拳心向上；右鉤手變拳，向前、向上掄臂，拳眼向左，拳心向左，兩拳高與胯平；目視右方。（圖 23）

挿
捶
套
路
動
作
圖
解

(1) Follow the above posture, the left foot lands firmly, the body lifts slightly and turns to the left. At the same time, swing the left arm downward and backward, with the fist –palm up; change the right hook hand into fist and swing arm forward and upward, with the fist–hole up, the fist–palm leftward. Keep two fists at hips height. Eyes look rightward. (Figure 23)

圖 24

(2)上動不停。身體右轉 180°，右腳向前跨半步，左腳隨即跟步，重心前移；同時，右拳隨身向右、向後掄臂；左臂向上、向前掄臂，兩臂成水平，右拳眼向後，拳心向下；左拳眼向上，拳心向右；目視左拳。（圖 24）

(2) Keep the above action, the body turns 180° to the left, the right foot strides half a step forward, then the left foot follows up, shift barycenter forward. At the same time, swing the right arm inward and backward with the body turn; the left arm swings upward and forward. Two arms shall be horizontal, with the right fist – hole backward and the fist – palm down; the left fist – hole upward and the fist – palm rightward. Eyes look at the left fist.（Figure 24）

挿捶套路動作圖解

圖 25

(3)上動不停。右腳向前上半步，左腳跟步，隨即左轉身 90°，身體下蹲成馬步；左拳向後收抱於腰間，拳心向上；右臂屈肘，右拳從外向裏圈擊，拳心向下，拳面向左；目視右方。（圖 25）

(3) Keep the above action, the right foot takes a half – step and the left one follows up, then the body turns to the left by 90°, the body squats into the horse stance. Draw back the left fist and hold on the waist, with the fist–palm up; bend elbow of the right arm, the right fist strikes circularly inward from outside, with the fist–palm down, the fist–plane leftward. Eyes look rightward. (Figure 25)

圖 26

12. 掄劈砸拳　Swing, chop and pound with fist

(1)接上勢。身體右轉 90°，右腳向前上半步，左腳隨即跟步，重心前移；同時，右拳隨身向上、向後掄臂，置於身右後方，拳眼向下；左拳從後向上、向前掄劈，拳心向右，拳眼向上，兩臂成水平；目視左拳。（圖 26）

挿捶套路動作圖解

(1) Follow the above posture, the body turns 90° to the left, the right foot takes half a step forward, the left one follows up, shift the barycenter forward. At the same time, swing the right arm upward and backward with the body turn and put the right fist at right back of the body, with the fist–hole down; the left fist swings upward and forward from back, with the fist–palm rightward, the fist–hole up. Two arms shall be horizontal. Eyes look at the left fist. (Figure 26)

七星螳螂拳　插捶

圖 27

（2）上動不停。右腳向前上半步，左腳跟步，隨即左轉身 90°，身體下蹲成馬步；同時，右拳從後向上掄起，隨轉身向右劈砸，拳眼向上，高與肩平；左拳向左、向上掄臂架拳於頭左上方，拳心向上；目視右拳。（圖 27）

（2）Keep the above action, the right foot takes a half-step for ward and the left one follows up, then the body turns 90° to the left, the body squats into the horse stance. At the same time, the right fist swing upward from back and chop rightward, with the fist -hole up at the shoulder height; swing the left fist leftward and upward and put the fist above the head, with the fist-palm up. Eyes look at the right fist.（Figure 27）

圖 28

13. 插花掌　Ikebana palm

(1) 接上勢。身體右轉 90°，左腳向前上步，隨即右腳向後撤步；同時，左拳收抱於腰間，拳心向上；右拳變掌，經胸前向外摟抓變拳，拳心向下，拳眼向左；目視右拳。（圖 28）

(1) Follow the above posture, the body turns 90° to the right, the left foot steps forward, then the right one follows up. At the same time, hold the left fist on the waist, with the fist–palm up; change the right fist into palm, grab outward through the front of the chest into fist, with the fist –palm down, the fist –hole leftward. Eyes look at the right fist.（Figure 28）

七星螳螂拳　插捶

圖 29

(2)上動不停。身體右轉 90°，向下蹲身成半馬步；同時，右拳收抱於腰間，拳心向上；左拳變掌，從外向裏封抓變拳，拳心向下，拳眼向右；目視左拳。（圖 29）

(2) Keep the above action, the body turns 90° to the right, squat the body downward to become the squat stance. At the same time, hold the right fist on the waist, with the fist–palm up; change the left fist into palm, closely grab inward from outside and change into the fist, with the fist–palm down, the fist–hole rightward. Eyes look at the left fist.（Figure 29）

插捶套路動作圖解

圖 30

　（3）上動不停。身體左轉 90°，重心前移成左弓
步；同時，左拳屈臂回收於胸前；右拳變八字掌向前
推掌，掌心向前，虎口向上；左拳心向下，拳背貼於
右肘下；目視右掌。（圖 30）

　（3）Keep the above action, the body turns 90° to the right
shift the barycenter forward into the left bow stance. At the same
time, bend the left arm, and draw back the left fist in front of the
chest; change the right fist into the eight‒shape palm and push
the palm forward, with the palm forward, tiger´s mouth up, with
the left fist‒palm down, the fist‒back sticking under the right
elbow. Eyes look at the right palm.（Figure 30）

圖 31

14. 抹眉插掌撩陰腳
Smear eyebrow, insert palm and uppercut groin with foot

(1)接上勢。重心前移，左腳蹬地直立，右腳腳面繃直向前彈踢；同時，右掌變拳收抱於腰間，拳心向上；左拳變掌向前平切，掌刃向前，虎口向右；目視左掌。（圖 31）

插捶套路動作圖解

(1)Follow the above posture, shift the barycenter for–ward, the left foot jumps up from the ground to stand up, stretch the right instep tight to kick forward. At the same time, change the right palm into fist and hold on the waist, with the fist–palm up; change the left fist into palm and chop forward horizontally, with the palm edge forward, the tiger´s mouth rightward. Eyes look at the left palm. (Figure 31)

圖 32

(2)上動不停。右腿屈膝收回，成左獨立勢；同時，右拳變掌向前穿出，掌心向下，掌指向前，高與肩平；左掌變拳，屈臂回收於右肘下，拳心向下，拳面向右；目視右掌。（圖 32）

(2) Keep the above action, bend knee of the right leg and draw back with standing alone on the left leg. At the same time, change the right fist into palm and thread forward, with the palm down and the fingers forward at the shoulder height; change the left palm into fist, bend arm and draw back under the right elbow, with the fist –palm down, fist –palne rightward. Eyes look at the right palm.（Figure 42）

圖 33

15. 撲食　Spring on prey

(1)接上勢。右腳向左腳內側落步震腳，兩膝微屈；同時，左拳變掌，兩掌在胸前翻腕絞手，隨即兩掌變拳交叉於胸前，左拳心向下，右拳心向上；目視左拳。（圖 33）

(2)Follow the above posture, the right foot fall to the inner side of the left one and stamp it, bend two knees slightly. At the same time, change the left fist into palm, two palms turn wrists and twist hands in front of the chest, then change two palms into fists and cross in front of the chest, with the left fist－palm down and the right one up. Eyes look at the left palm.（Figure 33）

圖 34

(2)上動不停。身體右轉 90°，左腳向左鏟腿平仆成左仆步；同時，右拳收抱於腰間，拳心向上；左拳屈肘下按，置於左小腿內側，拳心向下，拳眼斜向右；目視左拳。（圖 34）

(2) Keep the above action, the body turns 90° to the right the left foot shovels kick and crouches forward into the left crouch stance. At the same time, hold the right fist on the waist, with the fist-plam up; the left fist bend elbow and push downward and put it at the inner side of the left shank, with the fist-palm up, the fist-hole rightward aslant. Eyes look at the left fist.（Figure 34）

圖 35

16. 摟打一捶   Brush and punch

接上勢。身體左轉 90°，重心前移成左弓步；同時，左手外摟變拳收抱於腰間，拳心向上；右拳向前平沖，拳心向下，拳眼向左，高與肩平；目視右拳。（圖35）

Follow the above posture, the body turns 90° to the right, move the barycenter into the left bow stance. At the same time, the left hand grabs outward to change into fist and hold on the waist, with the fist-palm up; the right fist punches forward horizontally, with the fist-palm down, the fist-hole leftward at the shoulder height. Eyes look at the right fist. (Figure 35)

圖 36

17. 轉身一捶
Turn body and thrust hammer

接上勢。身體右轉 180°，重心前移成右弓步；同時，右手外摟變拳收抱於腰間，拳心向上；左拳向前平沖，拳心向下，拳眼向右，高與肩平；目視左拳。（圖 36）

挿捶套路動作圖解

Follow the above posture, the body turns to 180° to the right, shift the bargcenter into the right bow stance. At the sametime, the right hand grabs outward to change into fist and hold on the waist, with the fist–plam up; the left fist strikes forward horizontally, with the fist–palm down, the fist–hole rightward at the shoulder height. Eyes look at the left fist. (Figure 36)

圖 37

18. 插步盤肘
Insert step and bend elbow

(1)接上勢。身體左轉 90°，左腿經右腿後向右插步；同時，右拳變掌向前下方推擺，掌心向左前方，掌指向下；左拳屈臂回收於右肘下，拳心向下，拳面向右；目視右掌。（圖 37、圖 37 附圖）

圖 37 附圖

(1) Follow the above posture, the body turns 90° to the right
the left leg inserts rightward through the back of the right leg. At
the same time, change the right fist into palm and push and
swing ahead down, with the palm toward left ahead, the fingers
down. Bend the left arm and draw back the left fist under the
right elbow, with fist–palm down and the fist–plane rightward.
Eyes look at the right palm. ﹝ Figure 37, Attached figure 37 ﹞

圖 38

（2）上動不停。重心後移至左腿，左膝微屈，右腿抬起蹬直，腳尖上勾；同時，右掌變拳收抱於腰間，拳心向上；左拳變掌向前推洗，掌心向右，掌指向前，高與肩平；目視左掌。（圖 38）

(2) Keep the above action, shift the barycenter back to the left leg, bend the left knee slightly, the right leg lifts up and stretches straightly, with the tiptoe up. At the same time, the right palm change into fist and hold on the waist, with the fist－palm up; left fist changes into palm, then pushes the palm with palm back rubbing the arm with the palm rightward, the fingers forward at the shoulder height. Eyes look at the left palm. （Figure 38）

圖 39

(3)上動不停。身體左轉 90°，右腳向後撤一步成
左弓步；同時，右臂屈肘向前盤肘；左掌向裏迎擊右
前臂外側；目視右肘尖。（圖 39）

(3) Keep the above action, the body turns 180° to the right
the, right foot takes a step backward into the left bow stance.
At the same time, bend elbow of the right arm to strike forward
with the elbow; the left palm counterpunches the outer side of
the right forearm inward. Eyes look at the right elbow tip.
（Figure 39）

圖 40

第三段　Section　Three

19. 劈挑栽捶
Chop, uppercut and insert hammer

（1）接上勢。身體右轉 180°，右膝提起成左獨立勢；同時，左掌向前探掌，掌心向右，掌指向前，高與肩平；右拳屈臂上抬於右耳側，拳心向前，拳面向裏；目視左掌。（圖 40）

(1) Follow the above posture, the body turns 180° to the right, lift the right knee into the posture of standing alone. At the same time, the left palm stretches forward, with the fist –palm inward, the fingers forward at the shoulder level; bend the right arm and lift the right fist at the ear side, with the fist –palm forward, the fist –plane inward. Eyes look at the left palm. (Figure 40)

圖 41

(2)上動不停。右腳向前落地，左膝微屈；同時，右臂向前掄臂砸拳，拳輪向下；左掌向上迎擊右前臂內側，置於右胸前，掌心向右，掌指向上；目視右拳。（圖 41）

(2) Keep the above action, the right foot lands for–ward, bend the left knee slightly. At the same time, the right arm swings forward, poundes downward, with the fist–wheel down; the left palm counterpunches the inner side of the right forearm inward and put it in front of the chest, with the palm rightward, the fingers up. Eyes look at the right palm.（Figure 41）

挿捶套路動作圖解

圖 42

(3)上動不停。左腳向前上一步，右腳在後，左腳在前，重心在兩腿間；同時，左掌劃弧前探，掌心向右，掌指向前，高與肩平；右拳屈臂上抬於右耳側，拳心向下；目視左掌。（圖 42）

(3) Keep the above action, the left foot takes a step forward, with the right foot ahead and the left one back, the barycenter between two legs. At the same time, the left palm draws a curve and stretches forward, with the palm rightward and the fingers forward at the shoulder height; bend the right arm and lift the right fist at ears side, with the fist-palm down. Eyes look at the left palm. (Figure 42)

圖 43

(4)上動不停。右腳向前上一步，左腿屈膝，右腳
尖翹起成七星步；同時，右拳向前下方栽擊，拳眼向
左，拳面斜向下；左掌向上迎擊右前臂，掌心貼於右
肘內側，掌指向上；目視右拳。（圖 43）

(4) Keep the above action, the right foot takes a step
forward, bend knee of the left leg, with the right tiptoes up into
the seven-star step. At the same time, the right palm punches
downward, with the palm hole leftward, the fist-plane
downward aslant; the left palm counterpunches the right forearm
upward, with the palm sticking to the inner side of the right
elbow and the fingers up. Eyes look at the right fist.〔Figure
43〕

插捶套路動作圖解

圖 44

20. 上步雙封圈捶
Step forward, close up hands and circle hammer

(1)接上勢。右腳向後移半步踏實，隨即左腳上一步，身體右轉 90°；同時，兩手隨身向右封抓於小腹前，兩拳眼相對，拳心向下；目視兩拳。（圖 44）

(1) Follow the above posture, move the right foot back a half-step and land firmly, then the left foot takes a step forward, the body turns to the right by 90°. At the same time, two hands wraps rightward with the body fall before the lower abdomen, with two fist-holes opposite, the fist-palms downward. Eyes look at the two fists.（Figure 44）

七星螳螂拳 插捶

圖 45

（2）上動不停。身體左轉 90°，重心前移成左高弓步；同時，右拳屈肘向裏圈擊，拳面向右，拳心向下，高與肩平；左拳變掌，向外、向裏劃弧迎擊右前臂內側，掌心向外，掌指向上；目視前方。（圖 45）

（2）Keep the above action, the body turns 90° to the right. Move the barycenter into left high bow step. At the same time, the right fist draws a curve outward, then bend elbow for inward circular punch, with the fist-plane rightward, the fist-palm down at the shoulder level; change the left fist into palm and draw a curve outward and inward and counterpunch the inner side of the right forearm inward, with the palm outward, the fingers upward. Eyes look forward. (Figure 45)

插捶套路動作圖解

圖 46

21. 裏摟採三手
Brush inward and grab hand three times

（1）接上勢。步型不變；右拳變掌，向外、向上翻腕劃弧，隨即向裏摟手變拳，拳心向下，拳面向左，高與肩平；目視前方。（圖 46）

(1)Follow the above posture, keep the step unch-angeable, change the right fist into palm and turn wrist outward and upward and draw a curve, then grab inward and change into fist, with the fist-palm down, the fist-plane leftward at the shoulder height. Eyes look forward.（Figure 46）

圖 47

（2）上動不停。右拳收抱於腰間，拳心向上；同時，左掌向前、向裏摟採成拳，拳心向下，高與肩平；目視前方。（圖 47）

（2）Keep the above action, draw back the right fist and hold on the waist, with the fist–palm up. At the same time, the left palm forward inward grabs into fist, with the fist–palm down, at the shoulder level. Eyes look forward.（Figure 47）

圖 48

（3）上動不停。右拳自腰間經左拳上方向前沖拳，拳心向下，拳面向前，高與肩平；同時，左掌變拳，屈臂回收於右肘下，拳心向下，拳面向右；目視右拳。（圖 48）

(3) Keep the above action, the right fist strikes forward through the upper part of the left fist from the waist, with the fist-palm down, the fist-plane at the shoulder level. At the same time, change the left palm into fist and bend arm and draw back under the right elbow, with the fist-palm downward, the fist-plane rightward. Eyes look at the right palm.（Figure 48）

圖 49

22. 撩陰腳　uppercut-groin foot

接上勢。兩拳同時變掌向前平伸，左掌心向上，右掌心向下，兩掌略高於肩；同時，身體重心前移，左腿獨立，右腿向前彈踢；目視兩掌。（圖 49）

Follow the above posture, change two fists into palms simultaneously and stretch forward horizontally, with the left palm up, the right palm down, two palms higher than the shoulders slightly. At the same time, shift the barycenter of the body forward, the left leg stands alone, the right one kicks forward. Eyes look at two palms.（Figure 49）

圖 50

23. 順手牽羊 Lead away a goat in passing

接上勢。身體右轉 90°，右腳向右側落步，蹲身成
馬步；同時，兩手抓握變拳，隨轉身向右側回帶，左
拳心向右，拳眼向上；右拳眼向前，拳心向下，兩拳
高與胯平；目視右下方。（圖50）

Follow the above posture, the body turns 90° to the right.
The right foot lands down rightward, the body squats into the
horse stance. At the same time, clench two hands and change
into fists, turn the body to the right and pull back, with the left
fist–palm inward, the fist–hole up; the right fist–hole forward,
the fist–palm down, keep two fists at the hips level. Eyes look
right down. ﹝Figure 50﹞

圖 51

24. 左右圈捶　Left and right circular hammer

(1)接上勢。身體跳起向左轉 180°，兩腳互換仍成馬步；同時，右臂屈肘，右拳隨身向左圈擊，拳心向下，拳面向左，略低於肩；左拳隨身向左後方掄臂擺拳，拳眼向下；目視右方。（圖 51）

(1) Follow the above postue, the body jumps up and tums 180° tothe left, two feet interchande still to be horse stance. At the same time, bend the right arm, the right fist beats leftward circularly with the body tum, with the fist –palm down, fist –plane leftward, lower thanthe shoulder slightly; the left arm swings toward left back with the body turn, with the fist –hole down. Eyes look rightward. (Figure 51)

插捶套路動作圖解

圖 52

(2)上動不停。身體跳起向右轉 180°，兩腳互換仍成馬步；同時，左臂屈肘，左拳隨身向右圈擊，拳心向下，拳面向右，略低於肩；右拳隨身向右後方掄臂擺拳，拳眼向下；目視左方。（圖 52）

(2)Keep the above action, the body jumps up and turns 180° to the left, two feet interchange still to be the horse stance. At the same time, bend the right arm, the left fist thrusts leftward circularly with the body turn, with the fist–palm down, the fist–palm rightward, lower than the shoulder slightly; the left arm swings toward left back with the body turn, with the fist –hole down. Eyes look leftward.（Figure 52）

圖 53

25. 摟打一捶
Brush and punch

　　接上勢。身體左轉 90°，重心前移成左弓步；同時，左拳變掌外摟，隨即抓握變拳收抱於腰間，拳心向上；右拳隨身向前平沖，拳心向下，拳面向前，高與肩平；目視右拳。（圖 53）

挿捶套路動作圖解

Follow the above posture, the body turns 90° to the left, transfer the barycenter forward into the left bow step. At the same time, change the left fist into palm to grab outward, then clench it to change into fist and hold on the waist, with the fist – palm up; the right fist strikes forward horizontally with the body, with the fist –palm down and the fist –plane forward at the shoulder level. Eyes look at the right fist. (Figure 53)

圖 54

26. 虎抱頭劈砸
Tiger holds head with chop and pound

　　⑴接上勢。身體提起，重心前移，左腿獨立，右腳向前蹬出；同時，右臂屈肘經胸前向上抬起，架拳於頭右上方，拳面向前，拳眼向下；左拳變掌從腰間向前平推，掌心向前，掌指向上，高與肩平；目視左掌。（圖 54）

插捶套路動作圖解

(1) Follow the above posture, the body lifts up, mo – ve the barycenter forward, the left leg stands alone, the right foot kicks forward with heel. At the same time, bend elbow of the right arm and lift up through the front of the chest and put it above the head, with the fist – plane forward, the fist – hole down; change the left fist into palm and push forward horizontally from the waist, with the palm forward, the fingers upward at the shoulder height. Eyes look at the left palm. (Figure 54)

圖 55

　　(2)上動不停。身體左轉 90°，右腳落地，身體下蹲成馬步；同時，右拳掄起向身體右側砸拳，置於右膝外上方，拳輪向下，拳心向前，高與胯平；左掌從下向上迎擊右前臂，掌心貼於右肘關節內側，掌指向上；目視右拳。（圖 55）

插捶套路動作圖解

(2) Keep the above action, the body turns 90° to the right. The right foot falls to the ground, the body squats into the horse stance. At the same time, the right fist swings and pounds toward the right side of the body, and put it above outside the right knee, with the fist –wheel down, the fist –palm forward at the hip level; the left palm counterpunches the right forearm from down to up, with the palm sticking to the inner side of the right elbow joint, the fingers up. Eyes look at the right palm. (Figure 55)

圖 56

27. 白鶴亮翅
White crane spreads wings

(1)接上勢。身體提起，略微右轉，重心前移，左腳向右腳前方上步，腳尖外擺成蓋步；同時，右拳變掌，並屈臂抱於胸前，掌心向裏，掌指向左；左掌屈臂環抱於右臂外側，掌心向下，掌指向右；目視右方。（圖56、圖56附圖）

圖 56 附圖

(1)Follow the above posture, the body lifts up sli–ghtly and turns to the right, shift the barycenter forward, the left foot steps to the front of the right one, with the tiptoes swinging outward into the front cross stance. At the same time, change the right fist into palm, bend the arm and hold before the chest, with the palm inward and the fingers leftward. Bend the left arm and hold the left palm at the outer side of the right arm, with the palm down and the fingers rightward. Eyes look rightward.（Figure 56, Attached figure 56）

圖 57

(2)上動不停。左腿蹬地直立，右腿抬起，以腳尖
向右上方點擊；同時，右掌自胸前向右上方擺掌，掌
心向前，掌指向右，略高於肩；左掌掌心向裏，仍護
於右胸前；目視右腳尖。（圖 57）

(2)Keep the above action, the left leg kicks the gr–ound and
stands up, the right leg lifts up with the tiptoes striking right
upward. At the same time, the right palm swings right upward
through the front of the chest, with the palm forward and the
fingers rightward, higher than the shoulders slightly; with the left
palm inward, still guard in front of the chest. Eyes look at the
right tiptoes.（Figure 57）

圖 58

28. 轉身十字手
Turn body and cross hands

(1)接上勢。身體左轉 90°，右腳向身前落步；兩掌姿勢不變；目視右掌。（圖 58）

(1)Follow the above posture, the body turns 90° to the left and the right foot lands forward. Keep the palms unchangeable. Eyes look at the right palm.（Figure 58）

圖 59

(2)上動不停。左掌向前外摟變拳，拳心向下，拳眼向右，高與肩平；右掌變拳收抱於腰間，拳心向上；目視前方。（圖 59）

(2) Keep the above action, the left palm stretches for–ward for outward grab and change into fist, with the fist–palm down and the fist–hole rightward at the shoulder height; change the right palm into fist and hold on the waist, with the fist–palm up. Eyes look forward.（Figure 59）

圖 60

(3)上動不停。左腿提膝，左腳向右上方蹬出；同時，左拳收抱於腰間；右拳立拳向前平沖，拳心向左，拳面向前；目視右拳。（圖 60）

(3) Keep the above action, lift the knee of the left leg, the left foot kicks right upward. At the same time, draw back the left fist and hold on the waist; the right fist punches forward horizontally with the thumb side up, with the fist–palm leftward and the fist–plane forward. Eyes look at the right fist. 〔Figure 60〕

圖 61

29. 七星捶　Seven-star hammer

(1)接上勢。左腳向身左側落步，重心移至兩腿間；同時，右拳收抱於腰間，拳心向上；左拳變掌向前插出，掌心向右，掌指向前，高與肩平；目視左掌。（圖 61）

(1)Follow the above posture, the left foot lands to the left of the body and transfer the barycenter between two legs. At the same time, draw back the right fist and hold on the waist, with the fist–palm up; change the left fist into palm to insert forward, with the palm rightward and the fingers forward at the shoulder level. Eyes look at the left palm.〔Figure 61〕

圖 62

（2）上動不停。左腿屈膝，右腳上步，腳尖翹起成
七星步；同時，右拳立拳向前平沖，拳心向左，拳面
向前；左臂屈肘，左掌向右迎擊右拳面，左掌附於右
肘內側，掌心向右，掌指向上；目視右拳。（圖 62）

（2）Keep the above action, bend the knee of the left leg, the
right foot steps forward with the tiptoe up to change into the
seven –star stance. At the same time, the right standing fist
punches forward horizontally, with the palm side leftward and
the fist–plane forward; bend elbow of the left arm, the left palm
counterpunches the fist–plane inward, attach the left palm to the
inner side of the right elbow, with the palm rightward and the
fingers up. Eyes look at the right fist.（Figure 62）

圖 63

第四段　Section Four

30. 摟打躍步捶
Brush and punch with jumping step

⑴接上勢。右腳向前上步，左腳隨即跟步，重心前移成蹬山步；同時，右拳變掌外摟，再變拳收抱於腰間，拳心向上；左掌變拳，向前立拳沖出，拳心向右，拳面向前，高與肩平；目視左拳。（圖 63）

插捶套路動作圖解

(1)Follow the above posture, the right foot steps for−ward, then the left one follows up, shift the barycenter forward into mountaineer step. At the same time, change the right fist into palm and grab outward, change the palm into fist, draw it back and hold on the waist with the fist −palm up; change the left palm into fist and strike forward with the thumb side up, keep the fist −palm rightward and the fist −plane forward at the shoulder level. Eyes look at the left fist.〔Figure 63〕

七
星
螳
螂
拳

插
捶

圖 64

(2)上動不停。左腳向前上一步，隨即右腳跟步，
仍成蹬山步；同時，左拳變掌外摟，隨即變拳收抱於
腰間；右拳立拳向前平沖，拳眼向上，高與肩平；目
視右拳。（圖 64）

(2)Keep the above action, the left foot takes a step forward,
then the right one follows up into mountaineer stance. At the
same time, change the left fist into palm and grab it outward,
then change the palm into fist, draw it back and hold on the
waist; the right fist strikes forward horizontally with the thumb
side up and the fist-hole up at the shoulder height. Eyes look at
the right fist.〔Figure 64〕

圖 65

（3）上動不停。右腳向前上步，左腳隨即跟步，仍
成蹬山步；同時，右拳變掌外摟，再變拳收抱於腰
間，拳心向上；左拳向前立拳沖出，拳心向右，拳面
向前，高與肩平；目視左拳。（圖 65）

(3) Keep the above action, the right foot steps for – ward,
then the left one follows up into mountaineering step. At the
same time, change the right fist into palm and grab it outward,
change the palm into fist, draw it back and hold on the waist with
the fist – palm up; change the left fist strike forward with thumb
side up, keep the fist – palm rightward and the fist – plane forward
at the shoulder height. Eyes look at the left fist.（Figure 65）

圖 66

　　⑷上動不停。左腳向前上一步，隨即右腳跟步，
仍成蹬山步；同時，右拳立拳向前平沖，拳眼向上，
高與肩平；左拳變掌，附於右肘內側，掌心向右，掌
指向上；目視右拳。（圖 66）

　　⑷Keep the above action, the left foot takes a step forward,
then the right one follows up into mountaineering step. At the
same time, the right fist strikes forward horizontally with thumb
side up and the fist–hole upward at the shoulder level; change
the left fist into palm and attach to the inner side of the right
elbow with the palm rightward and the fingers up. Eyes look at
the right fist.（Figure 66）

圖 67

31. 左封右崩捶
Left wrap and right snap hammer

(1)接上勢。右腳向前上一步，隨即左腳跟步成蹬
山步；左手在胸前封抓變拳，拳心向下，拳面向右，
高與肩平；右拳收抱於腰間，拳心向上；目視前方。
（圖 67）

(1) Follow the above posture, the right foot takes a step
forward, then the left foot follows up into moun‒taineering step.
The left hand grabs into fist in front of the chest, keep the fist‒
palm down and the fist‒plane rightward at the shoulder height;
draw back the right fist and hold on the waist with the fist‒palm
up. Eyes look forward.（Figure 67）

七星螳螂拳　插捶

圖 68

(2)上動不停。重心略向前移；右拳拳心向左、向前崩拳，拳背向前，拳面向上，高與頜平；左拳置於右肘下，拳心向下；目視右拳。（圖 68）

(2) Keep the above action, slightly move the baryc –enter forward, the right fist snaps punch forward with the fist –palm leftward, keep the fist–back forward and the fist–plane up at the chin height; place the left fist under the right elbow with the fist–palm down. Eyes look at the right fist.〔Figure 68〕

插捶套路動作圖解

圖 69

32. 彎弓射虎　Bend bow to shoot the tiger

接上勢。步型不變，身體略向右擰；同時，右拳屈肘回帶，拳心向下，拳眼向左；左拳向左前方平沖，拳心向下，兩拳高與肩平；目視左拳。（圖 69）

Follow the above posture, keep the step unchangeable, twist the body rightward slightly. At the same time, bend the right elbow to bring back the right fist with the fist–palm down and the fist–hole leftward; the left fist strikes left forward horizontally with the fist–palm down. The two fists shall be at the shoulder height.Eyes look at the left fist.〔Figure 69〕

圖 70

33. 劈拳　Chop with the fist

接上勢。身體微向左轉；右拳從右向左前方斜劈，拳心向左，拳眼向上，高與肩平；左拳變掌迎擊右前臂內側，掌心貼於右肘內側；目視右拳。（圖70）

Follow the above posture, slightly turn the body to the left, hack the right fist aslant from right to left forward, keep the fist–palm leftward and the fist –hole up at the shoulder height; change the left fist into palm and counterpunch the inner side of the right forearm, keep the palm sticking to the inner side of the right elbow. Eyes look at the right fist.（Figure 70）

圖 71

34. 左封右崩捶
Left wrap and right snap hammer

(1)接上勢。身微右轉；左手在胸前封抓變拳，拳心向下，拳面向右，高與肩平；右拳收抱於腰間，拳心向上；目視前方。（圖 71）

(1) Follow the above posture, slightly turn the body to the right, the left hand grabs in front of the chest into fist, keep the fist –palm down and the fist –plane rightward at the shoulder height; draw back the right fist and hold on the waist with the fist–palm up. Eyes look forward.（Figure 71）

圖 72

（2）上動不停。重心略向前移；右拳拳心向左、向前崩拳，拳背向前，拳面向上，高與頜平；左拳置於右肘下，拳心向下；目視右拳。（圖 72）

（2）Keep the above action, move the barycenter for–ward slightly, the right fist snaps punch forward with the fist–palm leftward, the fist–back forward and the fist–plane up at the chin level; place the left fist under the right elbow with the fist–palm down. Eyes look at the right fist.〔Figure 72〕

插捶套路動作圖解

圖 73

35. 雙封手　Close-up double hands

(1)接上勢。身體提起，左轉 180°，重心落於兩腿間；同時，右拳變掌，隨身向左劃弧，兩掌交叉於腹前，右掌在外，左掌在裏，兩掌心均向下；目視兩掌。（圖 73）

(1) Follow the above posture, raise the body and turn 180° to the left, keep the barycenter between the two legs. At the same time, change the right fist into palm and draw a curve leftward with the body, cross the two palms in front of the abdomen, with the right palm outside, the left one inside, and the two palms down. Eyes look at the two palms. (Figure 73)

圖 74

　　(2)上動不停。身體略向後傾斜；同時，兩臂屈肘，兩掌在胸前翻轉絞手，右掌心向上，掌指向右，左掌心向右，兩掌高與頷平；目視兩掌。（圖 74）

　　(2) Keep the above action, lean the body slightly backward. At the same time, bend the two elbows, turn over the two palms and twist the hands in front of the chest with the right palm up and the fingers rightward, and the left palm rightward. The two palms shall be at the chin height. Eyes look at the two palms. （Figure 74）

插捶套路動作圖解

圖 75

(3)上動不停。重心略前移；同時，右掌前探，掌心向前，虎口向上，高與肩平；左掌護於右肩前，掌指向上，掌心向右；目視右掌。（圖 75）

(3) Keep the above action, shift the barycenter for –ward slightly. At the same time, the right palm stretches forward, with the palm forward, the tiger´s mouth up, at the shoulder height; the left palm guards in front of the right shoulder with the fingers up and the palm rightward. Eyes look at the right palm. ﹝ Figure 75 ﹞

圖 76

(4)上動不停。右臂屈肘，右掌變為螳螂鉤，吊腕勾拉於胸前，鉤尖向下；同時，左掌向前探，掌心向左，掌指向前，高與肩平；目視左掌。（圖 76）

(4) Keep the above action, bend the right elbow, change the right palm into mantis hook, hang the wrist and draw to the front of the chest with the hook－tip downward. At the same time, the left palm stretches forward, with the palm leftward and the fingers forward at the shoulder height. Eyes look at the left palm.（Figure 76）

圖 77

(5)上動不停。身體下蹲；同時，左臂屈肘，左鉤
手吊腕回拉於左膝上方，略低於肩；目視左前方。
（圖 77）

(5) Keep the above action, the body squats. At the same
time, bend the left elbow, hang the wrist of the left hook hand
and draw back upon the left knee, lower than the shoulder
slightly. Eyes look left forward.（Figure 77）

圖 78

36. 收勢　Closing form

（1）接上勢。身體右轉 90°成馬步；同時，兩鉤手
變掌，經胸前上托，隨即向兩側分掌，兩臂成水平，
兩掌心向外，掌指向上；目視右掌。（圖 78）

（1）Follow the above posture, turn the body to the right by
90° into the horse stance. At the same time, change the two hook
hands into palms and lift them up through the front of the chest,
then part the palms to both sides of the body. The two arms shall
be at the same level, with the two palms outward and the fingers
up. Eyes look at the right palm.（Figure 78）

圖 79

(2)上動不停。身體重心提起，左腳向右腳併步；
同時，兩掌變拳抱於腰間；目視前方。（圖 79）

(2) Keep the above action, raise the barycenter, bring the
left foot to the right one. At the same time, change the two palms
into fists and hold on the waist. Eyes look forward.（Figure
79）

圖 80

(3)上動不停。兩拳變掌，自然下垂於身體兩側；目視前方。（圖 80）

要點：挺胸收腹，平心靜氣，體態自然，精神內斂。

(3) Keep the above action, change two fists into palms and drop naturally at both sides of the body. Eyes look forward. （Figure 80）

Key points: Lift the chest, draw in the abdomen, calmly, posture is natural and vital energy collects inward.

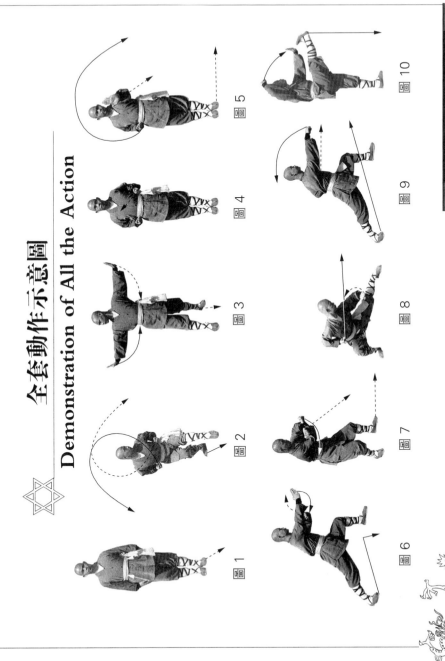

全套動作示意圖

Demonstration of All the Action

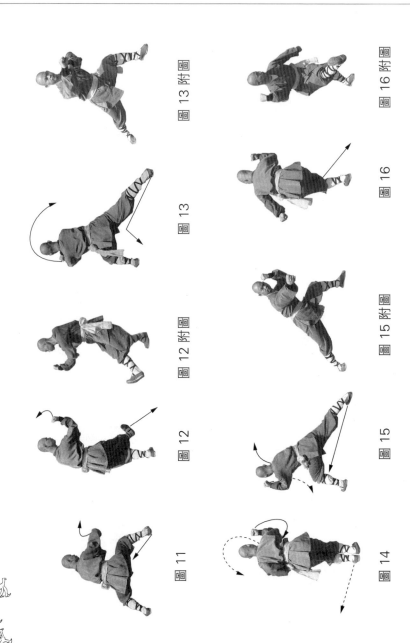

七星螳螂拳　插捶

图 13 附图

图 13

图 12 附图

图 12

图 11

图 16 附图

图 16

图 15 附图

图 15

图 14

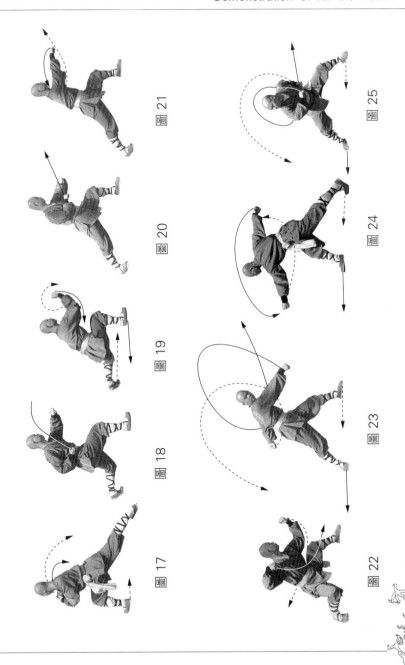

全套動作示意圖

圖 21

圖 20

圖 19

圖 18

圖 17

圖 25

圖 24

圖 23

圖 22

七星螳螂拳　插捶

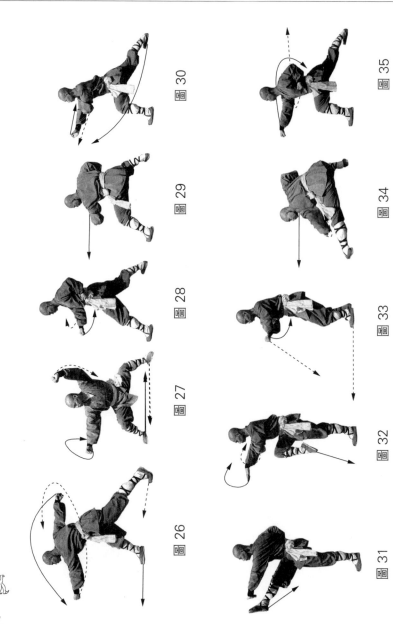

图 30

图 29

图 28

图 27

图 26

图 35

图 34

图 33

图 32

图 31

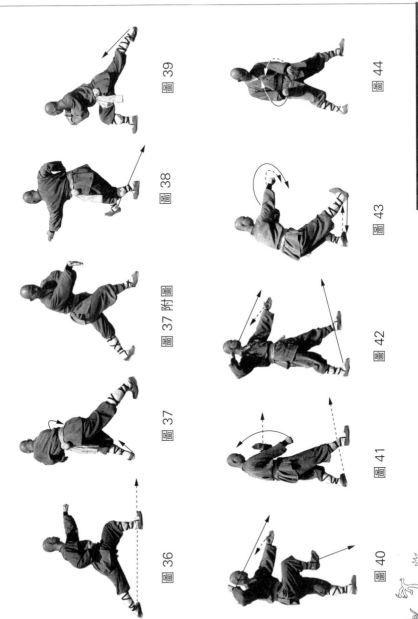

全套動作示意圖

圖 39 圖 38 圖 37 附圖 圖 37 圖 36

圖 44 圖 43 圖 42 圖 41 圖 40

七星螳螂拳　插捶

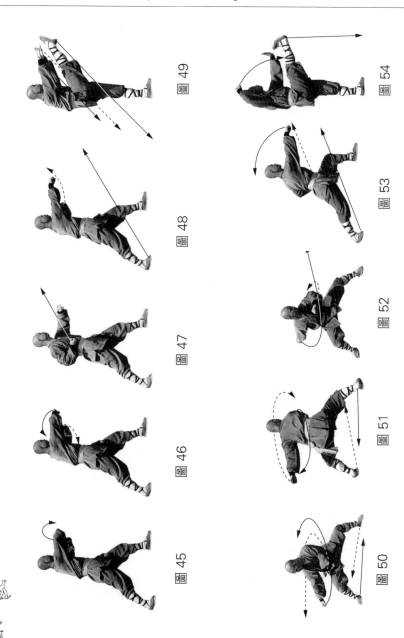

圖 49

圖 48

圖 47

圖 46

圖 45

圖 54

圖 53

圖 52

圖 51

圖 50

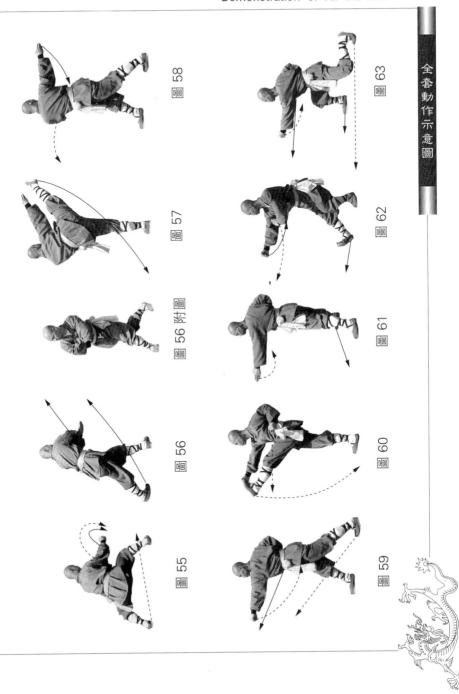

圖 58

圖 57

圖 56 附圖

圖 56

圖 55

圖 63

圖 62

圖 61

圖 60

圖 59

全套動作示意圖

图 67

图 66

图 65

图 64

图 71

图 70

图 69

图 68

全套動作示意圖

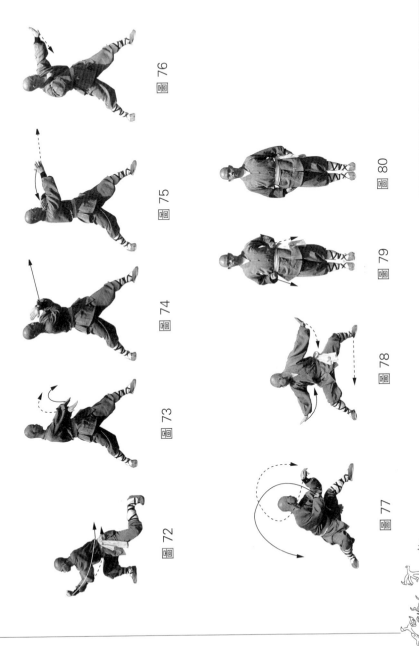

圖 76

圖 75

圖 74

圖 73

圖 72

圖 80

圖 79

圖 78

圖 77

導引養生功 系列叢書

- ◎ 1. 疏筋壯骨功
- ◎ 2. 導引保健功
- ◎ 3. 頤身九段錦
- ◎ 4. 九九還童功
- ◎ 5. 舒心平血功
- ◎ 6. 益氣養肺功
- ◎ 7. 養生太極扇
- ◎ 8. 養生太極棒
- ◎ 9. 導引養生形體詩韻
- ◎ 10. 四十九式經絡動功

張廣德養生著作

每冊定價 350 元

全系列為彩色圖解附教學光碟

彩色圖解太極武術

1 太極功夫扇
定價220元

2 武當太極劍
定價220元

3 楊式太極劍
定價220元

4 楊式太極刀
定價220元

5 二十四式太極拳＋VCD
定價350元

6 三十二式太極劍＋VCD
定價350元

7 四十二式太極劍＋VCD
定價350元

8 四十二式太極拳＋VCD
定價350元

9 楊式十六式太極劍
定價350元

10 楊氏二十八式太極拳＋VCD
定價350元

11 楊式太極拳四十式＋VCD
定價350元

12 陳式太極拳五十六式＋VCD
定價350元

13 吳式太極拳五十六式＋VCD
定價350元

14 精簡陳式太極拳八式十六式
定價220元

15 精簡吳式太極拳三十六式拳架・推手
定價220元

16 夕陽美功夫扇
定價220元

17 綜合四十八式太極拳＋VCD
定價350元

18 三十二式太極拳四段
定價220元

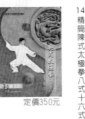

19 楊式三十七式太極拳＋VCD
定價350元

20 楊氏五十一式太極劍＋VCD
定價350元

太極跤

1 太極防身術

定價300元

2 擒拿術

定價280元

3 中國式摔角

定價350元

簡化太極拳

1 陳式太極拳十三式

定價200元

2 楊式太極拳十三式

定價200元

3 吳式太極拳十三式

定價200元

4 武式太極拳十三式

定價200元

5 孫式太極拳十三式

定價200元

6 趙堡太極拳十三式

定價200元

原地太極拳

1 原地綜合太極二十四式

定價220元

2 原地活步太極四十二式

定價200元

3 原地簡化太極拳二十四式

定價200元

4 原地太極拳十二式

定價200元

5 原地青少年太極拳二十二式

定價220元

6 原地兒童太極拳十種十六式

定價180元

國家圖書館出版品預行編目資料

七星螳螂拳　插捶／耿　軍　著
　　——初版，——臺北市，大展，2007〔民96〕
　　面；21 公分，——（少林傳統功夫漢英對照系列；4）
　　ISBN　978-957-468-532-5（平裝）

1. 拳術—中國
528.97　　　　　　　　　　　　　　　　　96003056

七星螳螂拳　插捶

ISBN－13：978-957-468-532-5

著　　者／耿　軍
責任編輯／孔 令 良
發 行 人／蔡 森 明
出 版 者／大展出版社有限公司
社　　址／台北市北投區（石牌）致遠一路 2 段 12 巷 1 號
電　　話／（02）28236031・28236033・28233123
傳　　眞／（02）28272069
郵政劃撥／01669551
網　　址／www.dah-jaan.com.tw
E－mail／service@dah-jaan.com.tw
登 記 證／局版臺業字第 2171 號
承 印 者／高星印刷品行
裝　　訂／建鑫印刷裝訂有限公司
排 版 者／弘益電腦排版有限公司
授 權 者／北京人民體育出版社
初版 1 刷／2007 年（民 96 年）5 月

定　價／180 元

一億人閱讀的暢銷書！

4 ～ 26 集　定價300元　特價230元

4.大金塊　　5.青銅魔人　　6.地底魔術王　　7.透明怪人　　8.怪人四十面相　　9.宇宙怪人

.恐怖的鐵塔王國　11.灰色巨人　12.海底魔術師　13.黃金豹　14.魔法博士　15.馬戲怪人

6.魔人銅鑼　17.魔法人偶　18.奇面城的秘密　19.夜光人　20.塔上的魔術師　21.鐵人Q

.假面恐怖王　23.電人M　24.二十面相的詛咒　25.飛天二十面相　26.黃金怪獸

品冠文化出版社

地址：臺北市北投區
　　　致遠一路二段十二巷一號
電話：〈02〉28233123
郵政劃撥：19346241